THE NATIONAL
GRAPE BOYCOTT

A Victory for Farmworkers

by Barbara J. Davis

THE NATIONAL GRAPE BOYCOTT

A Victory for Farmworkers

by Barbara J. Davis

Content Adviser: Derek Shouba, Adjunct
History Professor, Roosevelt University

Reading Adviser: Katie Van Sluys, Ph.D.,
School of Education, DePaul University

Compass Point Books ◆ Minneapolis, Minnesota

COMPASS POINT BOOKS

3109 West 50th Street, #115
Minneapolis, MN 55410

Visit Compass Point Books on the Internet at
www.compasspointbooks.com
or e-mail your request to
custserv@compasspointbooks.com

For Compass Point Books
Jennifer VanVoorst, Brenda Haugen, Jaime Martens,
XNR Productions, Inc., Catherine Neitge, Keith Griffin,
Lori Bye, and Nick Healy

Produced by White-Thomson Publishing Ltd.

For White-Thomson Publishing
Stephen White-Thomson, Susan Crean, Amy Sparks,
Tinstar Design Ltd., Derek Shouba, Peggy Bresnick Kendler,
Barbara Bakowski, and Timothy Griffin

Library of Congress Cataloging-in-Publication Data
Davis, Barbara J., 1952–
  The National grape boycott : a victory for farmworkers / by
Barbara J. Davis.
      p. cm. — (Snapshots in history)
  ISBN-13: 978-0-7565-2454-8 (library binding)
  ISBN-10: 0-7565-2454-7 (library binding)
1. Chavez, Cesar, 1927—Juvenile literature. 2. Labor leaders—United
States—Biography—Juvenile literature. 3. Mexican American migrant
agricultural laborers—Biography—Juvenile literature. 4. United Farm
Workers—History—Juvenile literature. I. Title. II. Series.
  HD6509.C48D375 2008
  331.89'0433480973—dc22   2007004919

Contents

Taking a Stand

At the age of 20, Angie Hernandez Herrera had worked in the fields of Delano, California, for as long as she could remember. Everyone in her family did. They tended and harvested fields of cotton, vegetables, and fruits. So did Herrera's friends and their families. If you were Mexican or Filipino in the San Joaquin Valley town of Delano, you probably worked in somebody's fruit orchard, vineyard, or vegetable farm.

The work was difficult. Digging in the soil with short-handled hoes caused painful blisters on people's hands. Bending over for hours each day meant sore backs. The farmworkers labored from when the sun had barely risen in the sky to when it set for the day. Often this was 10 or 12 hours. For all their hard work, the farmworkers usually earned less than $1 an hour.

On one fateful day—March 17, 1966—Herrera and 70 other farmworkers planned to change their situation. It would take several weeks, but they were going to walk all the way from Delano to the California Capitol in Sacramento—almost 300 miles (480 kilometers). When they arrived, the farmworkers would ask the people of the United States to help them in their cause.

Entire families, including small children, worked long hours in the California fruit and vegetable fields.

9

The farmworkers wanted decent housing instead of rickety shacks or tin huts that baked them in the summer. They wanted to be able to get a drink of fresh water in the fields if they needed it. Most of the time, they could not leave their work, even to get a drink of water, regardless of how high the temperature rose.

Working stooped over in the fields, breathing the same poison they sprayed on the plants to kill bugs, the farmworkers were often sick. They needed some type of medical care to be available when they could no longer work. The farmworkers wanted to make enough money to be able to buy food for their families. They also wanted their children to have a chance to attend school.

As the marchers began to gather in the barrio, there was much laughing and joking. Herrera shared the excitement everyone felt. She later said, "We were right there on Albany Street, with the organizers trying to get us in line. ... It was like a big party."

Smaller children who would walk only part of the way were giggling as they darted in and out between the legs of the adults. The marchers, and even some children, wore red armbands in support of the idea of a farmworkers' union. Many marchers held up large pictures of the Virgin of Guadalupe, the patron saint of Mexico and the symbol of hope for the march. Others carried the flag of the United States or Mexico.

Above the marchers' heads, banners floated in the air. The banners represented the National Farm Workers Association (NFWA), an organization led by Cesar Chavez that fought for the rights of all farmworkers. The symbol of this new workers' union was a black eagle on a red background. When the banners moved, it looked as if the eagle were flying.

Even though most of the marchers were smiling, they were also nervous. These Filipino and Mexican workers had united in a strike against the fruit growers. The workers had walked off their jobs, leaving thousands of acres of unpicked fruit.

Union leader Cesar Chavez (right) led the marchers, who carried flags and banners on the long walk to Sacramento.

If the fruit did not get picked in time, it would rot in the fields, and the growers would lose significant amounts of money.

The marchers had no idea how the growers would attempt to stop their march to Sacramento. The farmworkers found out, however, as soon as they began the march. There, in front of them, a line of armed Delano police officers blocked their path.

Leading the march was Chavez. Herrera was walking beside Chavez as they approached the waiting police officers. Although Chavez had led the marchers through downtown Delano, they did not have a permit to be there. More than one marcher worried that there would be a violent clash.

The marchers did not carry any weapons. Chavez believed that the farmworkers must achieve their goals through nonviolence. The police, however, carried guns and clubs. The police chief knew that Chavez would not turn back. Tension was heavy in the air.

There were many newspaper and television reporters in Delano covering the march. The chief of police knew that if there was trouble, Americans all across the country would witness it.

The police chief and Chavez spoke. With the nation watching, the two leaders reached an agreement—the march would be allowed to

proceed, even though Chavez and his followers did not have a formal permit. The marchers cheered, waving their colorful flags and banners.

As the marchers moved down Highway 99 toward Sacramento, they began to grow tired. Their spirits were lifted, though, by the people they met along the way to the state Capitol. Farmworkers in the fields waved and called out as the marchers walked by. Some people joined the march for a few miles. Even those with very little were eager to share refreshments with the tired walkers. More than one family had sweet punch and tortillas for the marchers. They all wanted to be a part of this monumental event, even if they could not march themselves.

Marchers felt relieved that they were able to avoid a violent confrontation with Delano, California, police officers.

People all across the United States were able to watch the march's progress on television or read about it in the newspapers. They saw Chavez limping from the blisters that had formed on his feet. Despite the pain, he kept walking. Herrera walked right with him. Sometimes the people in the march walked as far as 15 miles (24 km) in a day. No matter what, the march kept going. Herrera was awed by the bravery she saw around her. She later recalled, "Some people had bloody feet. ... You'd see blood coming out of their shoes."

Finally, after more than three weeks of marching, the farmworkers approached Sacramento. Bone tired, with sore feet and muscles, the exhausted marchers hoped that all their efforts would be recognized. The crowd cheered loudly and waved small flags and banners. There were so many pieces of waving cloth that the sky appeared to be full of ribbons. A group of Mexican Americans on horseback carried flags as they led the weary marchers into Sacramento.

There were so many things the farmworkers needed, but they knew they could not get those things without help. The workers decided to seek the help of the American people who ate the food the farmworkers picked. At the time, Americans consumed about 700 million pounds (315 million kilograms) of table grapes each year. When the marchers arrived in Sacramento, they would ask Americans to stop eating grapes in support of the farmworkers' cause.

Why a Boycott?

If Americans stopped eating table grapes, the growers would not be able to sell as many to the grocery stores. That would cause the growers to lose a lot of money. It might also cause the growers to realize how important farmworkers were to the success of their businesses. Maybe then the growers would agree to the farmworkers' requests. To the farmworkers, asking the American people to boycott table grapes seemed like the best action to take.

Dolores Huerta was a leader of the farmworkers. She had worked closely with Chavez in organizing the farmworkers' union. When Huerta joined Chavez on the steps of the Capitol, she looked around at the farmworkers and the joyous crowd. The real work would lie ahead, she stated. To the owners of the large vineyards and fields, she said:

> *You cannot close your eyes and your ears to us any longer. You cannot pretend that we do not exist. You cannot plead ignorance to our problems because we are here and we embody our needs for you. And we are not alone!*

Herrera listened with great pride. She was a part of all of this—she and the generations of farmworkers before her. For the first time, the farmworkers had won the right to choose the union that would represent them to the growers. United in a union, the farmworkers had more power to change their lives. They had a chance to stand up to the growers—and win. ◣

Hard Work for Little Money

Migrant workers have been a part of California's farming history for almost 150 years. During the 1860s, wealthy business owners from around the country—including railroad barons, bankers, and industrialists—began buying thousands of acres of farmland in California. A great deal of money could be made, and these owners knew it. The country was quickly growing, and its people would have to be fed.

The climate along the Pacific Coast made many areas in the region particularly good for farming. Vegetables such as lettuce grew well there, and fruits such as strawberries and grapes also thrived. So much food could be produced in these areas that it seemed as if enough could be grown to feed the entire nation.

Migrant workers tended row after row of lettuce plants in the early days of the California agriculture industry.

MIGRANT WORKERS

California produces a wide variety of fruits and vegetables that are transported throughout the United States and to other countries. Much of the produce grown in California and other states is still largely harvested by hand. Each year, about 700,000 farmworkers travel from farm to farm to help harvest the produce. These farmworkers are called migrant workers because they migrate, or move, to follow the harvest of the fruits and vegetables that feed the nation.

At the time that the business owners were buying up the land, railroads were linking the different regions of the United States. In 1860, there were 30,000 miles (48,000 km) of railroad track laid throughout the United States. In 1869, the first transcontinental railroad was completed. By the 1880s, about 160,500 miles (256,800 km) of track crisscrossed the country.

Because of the railroads, fruits and vegetables grown in California and elsewhere could be shipped to almost any part of the country. Before the produce could be shipped, though, it had to be harvested from the fields. Growers needed farmworkers for the harvest.

There just happened to be a great source for these workers on hand—immigrants. Thousands of Chinese workers were already in the western territories and in California. They had helped lay the tracks for the railroad that stretched from one end of the country to the other. Many of

the Chinese immigrants who had worked on the railroad were now put to work in the olive groves, strawberry farms, and lettuce fields owned by wealthy American growers.

Chinese immigrants laid thousands of miles of railroad track in the United States.

The Chinese immigrants worked hard but earned little money. Even though they did the same backbreaking job as the other farmworkers, the Chinese immigrants were paid far less. One of the large growers wrote in a letter at the time that he paid Chinese workers $1 per day. Caucasian workers, however, earned $15 per day, in addition to food and lodging.

19

This same farm owner said later that he believed the Chinese immigrants did the best job of picking and packing the farm's fruit. The quality of the work done by the Chinese and the low pay they received meant more profit for the farm owner.

During the 1860s, the Chinese farmworkers began traveling through the state, following the harvests. They became the first migrant workers on which California's farming industry depended. Though the work they did brought large profits to farm owners, it did not translate to high wages for the farmworkers. Because they could not survive on the money they made in one place, migrant workers were constantly on the move, looking for their next jobs.

From the beginning, some landowners in California treated the Chinese immigrants as little more than slaves. Even though California did not permit slavery as it existed in the South, many white people in California had strong prejudices against those of other races. To them, the Chinese immigrants did not have the same rights as white people. In fact, they had no rights. Chinese workers could be beaten, or even killed, without any real consequences. If they were cheated of their wages, they could do little to right the wrong.

Despite the skillful job the immigrants did, harsh economic times in the 1870s led some people to complain that the Chinese were taking the work that rightfully belonged to white workers. As a result, many Chinese farmworkers lost their jobs. They were replaced by white farmworkers who had been steadily flowing into California to look for jobs. When the economy started to improve, however, these farmworkers moved on to different jobs. Suddenly, the growers needed large numbers of field workers to replace the Caucasians who had gone to better-paying or less labor-intensive jobs. The growers looked once more to immigrants.

In the 1880s, a new group of immigrants began arriving in California. These Japanese fishermen, farmers, and tradespeople brought with them particularly useful knowledge in a number of areas. Japanese farmers introduced certain planting and harvesting methods that resulted in even more plentiful crops. One farmer, for example, covered rows of early vegetables with a type of newspaper tent. This helped to reflect the sun's warmth on the plants while also protecting the young roots from frost. The landowners welcomed the new

THE CHINESE EXCLUSION ACT

The Chinese workers who had helped build the railroad were usually single men or men who had left their families in China. When these laborers began to work in the farm fields, wives and families arrived to join them. As the number of Chinese immigrants grew, some white citizens became concerned. In the 1870s, the United States went through an economic depression. This led some Americans to decide that there were too many Chinese immigrants and that they were taking jobs that should go to U.S. citizens. As a result, the U.S. government passed the Chinese Exclusion Act in 1882. While millions of Europeans were allowed to freely enter the United States at this time, the U.S. government kept strict limits on the number of Asians and other nonwhites allowed into the country.

arrivals. By the turn of the century, many thousands of Japanese immigrants had found work all along the Pacific Coast. The Japanese became the new migrant workers, following the harvests.

Like the Chinese migrant workers before them, Japanese farmworkers faced harsh working conditions. They were paid barely enough money to survive. As nonwhite immigrants, the Japanese had few rights under the law.

The racism shown to the Chinese immigrants carried over to the Japanese. Some white Americans soon reacted to the presence of the Japanese immigrants as they had toward the Chinese. These Americans felt there were just too many Japanese living in California. Eventually many Japanese immigrants bought or rented small farms of their own. They started businesses such as grocery and clothing stores to serve the Japanese community. This helped the Japanese immigrants build better lives. It also resulted in far fewer Japanese working in the fields than before.

The racist attitude of some Americans led to the restriction of Japanese immigration in 1908. In 1923, the Alien Land Law made it illegal for immigrants who could not become U.S. citizens to own land. Laws were already in place that made it impossible for Asian immigrants to become citizens. The new law applied not only to Asian immigrants who wanted to buy land but also to Asians who had bought land before the new law was passed. These people either lost their land or had to transfer ownership of the land to a non-Asian person.

As the Japanese tried to find better employment away from the fields, the growers were forced to look elsewhere for workers to tend fields and harvest crops. During the early 1900s, immigration laws were changed to make it easier for Mexican workers to enter the United States. Between 1917 and 1921, more than 23,000 Mexicans legally entered the United States. By the end of the 1920s, more than 70,000 Mexicans were living in California at least part of the year. Between 1923 and 1930, 23,000 Filipinos also went to California.

Because the Philippines was considered a U.S. colony, Filipinos could enter the United States

THE MEXICAN REVOLUTION

In 1910, Mexican rebels rose up to fight against the dictator José de la Cruz Porfirio Diás. The violent revolution changed Mexico's government and the Mexican people's way of life. The Mexican Revolution lasted 30 years. The constant fighting drove thousands of Mexicans across the border into the United States. The Mexican population in the United States grew from about 103,000 in 1900 to almost 1.5 million in 1940. Many of these immigrants settled in California, Texas, Arizona, and New Mexico. Many of the well-educated immigrants opened businesses to serve the growing Mexican community. Poorer, uneducated immigrants found work as farm laborers. In certain areas of California, such as the Imperial Valley, the majority of farmworkers were of Mexican descent.

without any restrictions. Labor contractors went to villages and towns in Mexico and the Philippines and told the townspeople that farmworkers were needed in the United States. The contractors said that the laborers could earn far more money there than in their own countries. Soon there were many new immigrants to work in the fields.

These workers came from extreme poverty. Even the $1 to $3 per day they received in wages was an improvement over what they had left behind in Mexico or the Philippines. Some of the Mexican immigrants had made as little as 16 cents a day back home. With so many workers willing to work for extremely low wages, the California farming industry grew even larger, and the landowners grew even richer.

The new migrant workers also faced racism. Even though the farming industry could not exist without the migrants' labor, many growers looked at the workers as lesser beings. A California sheriff said, "The Mexicans are trash. They have no standard of living. We herd them like pigs."

During the Great Depression of the 1930s, many Americans lost their jobs, homes, and life's savings. In California, as in other states, there were many more people than jobs. As a result, all the migrant workers—including white farmers known as Okies, who had traveled from the Midwest—competed with one another for whatever work could be had. Because there were so many workers, the growers could pay even less than they had before the Depression. People were willing to work for little, as long as they could earn something. Sometimes the pay was a bit of food or a place to sleep. Often a day's wage was just a few dollars.

Entire families worked from before dawn to dusk. Children as young as 5 years old worked in the fields alongside their parents. Young or old, the farmworkers often spent whole days stooped over weeding or harvesting low-growing plants. The

The promise of better wages encouraged poor Mexican migrant families looking for work to travel from farm to farm in California.

MIGRATION TO THE WEST

The 1930s brought the Great Depression to the United States. Tens of thousands of Americans lost everything they owned. The farm fields of the Great Plains were buried in dust from a long drought. Many of the farmers who owned those fields packed up what little they had left and headed west to California. The farmers who traveled west were called Okies because a large number of them had come from failed farms in Oklahoma. The Okies hoped to find jobs. Instead, they found disaster.

workers called strawberries the "fruit of the devil" because picking them was so painful. The workers' fingers bled, and many suffered permanent damage to their spines. Legs and feet were sometimes crushed by heavy barrels. Sharp farm tools easily sliced off fingers or hands. Chemicals used to fertilize the soil sometimes splashed into a farmworker's eyes and caused permanent loss of eyesight. Laborers faced all this danger and pain for about $3 a day.

Workers were paid by the amount of produce they could pick. Slowing down because of pain, hunger, or exhaustion wasn't an option. The laborers would pick as quickly as they could, run to get their baskets or boxes weighed, and then go back to the rows of produce and resume their work.

They were forced to live in tents made of ragged blankets or in huts made of cardboard and tin. In the summer, the tin shacks became as hot as ovens. Shoes were a luxury few workers could afford. Often whole families faced starvation. Some

migrant children died of malnutrition as their parents struggled to find work so they could buy food.

In some migrant camps, medical personnel attempted to deal with the problem of children facing malnutrition.

While all this misery was going on, the huge farms got even bigger. Small family farms that had been lost during the Depression became part of the larger farms that already existed in California. The businessmen who ran these huge farms often did not live in California. As the migrant workers suffered, the corporate farms grew even more profitable. ◪

Organizing Workers

The suffering of the migrant laborers became known to the rest of the United States through the efforts of writers, journalists, and artists. Photographers such as Dorothea Lange captured images of the migrants at work and in their humble shelters. Newspaper reporters began to write stories about the terrible conditions under which the migrant workers lived. John Steinbeck grew up in an area where migrant labor was common. As a reporter for the *San Francisco News*, he wrote a number of articles about the Oklahomans who lived as migrant workers.

Steinbeck was horrified by the misery he saw, and he reported it in detail. Steinbeck's articles painted a grim picture of a migrant worker's life. When he later became a novelist,

Dorothea Lange captured in images the lives of migrant workers in the 1930s and the makeshift homes in which they lived.

A Picture Is Worth 1,000 Words

Photographer Dorothea Lange used her camera to capture the suffering of the migrant workers who streamed into California during the Great Depression. Traveling from migrant camp to migrant camp, she took pictures to document the effects of the Great Depression on thousands of people. Her photographs recorded the sadness and hopelessness in the eyes of children and adults forced to live in horrible conditions. Those images also helped bring the story of the migrant workers to others across the nation. Lange's work encouraged U.S. government leaders and others to become more active in relieving the misery of the migrant camps.

he recounted what he had seen in the migrant labor camps in *The Grapes of Wrath*, a novel that was widely read among Americans.

While their story was being told around the country, most migrant workers made their own attempts to improve the conditions in which they worked and lived. For years, many migrants tried to organize into groups called unions that would try to negotiate with the growers for better wages and housing.

The farmworkers wanted contracts that would guarantee them a certain wage. They also wanted the contracts to spell out the responsibilities the growers had toward the workers, which included such basic things as providing drinking water to workers at all times. The workers also wanted the contracts to include guarantees of decent housing, as well as medical help if a worker was injured.

If the worker was so severely injured that he or she could no longer work, the unions wanted a plan that would help the worker's family survive. In forming these early unions, laborers were asking for nothing more than the basic necessities that all people should have.

Farmworkers found that forming unions helped them achieve better working and living conditions.

The members of early unions often came from a particular culture. For example, the Filipino Labor Union formed in 1933. Some migrants sought the support of existing unions, such as the American Federation of Labor (AFL). But the AFL membership was mostly made up of white workers. It would not help unions that had nonwhite members.

From the start, the unions met with strong resistance from the growers. The growers did not take the farmworkers' unions seriously or see them as real threats to business. Part of the reason for resistance was racism. Growers saw the nonwhite migrant workers as people who were incapable of making decisions or managing a union. A writer to a newspaper of the day wrote that the nonwhite farmworkers in the unions were "people whose experience has been only to obey a master rather than think and manage for themselves."

A UNION FOR ALL

The Industrial Workers of the World (IWW) was a union that tried to help all California immigrant farmworkers, regardless of ethnicity. The IWW organized strikes and pressured the growers to pay better wages. By 1917, more than 10,000 migrant field workers belonged to the IWW. The union championed the rights of workers of many races. Despite the large membership, the powerful growers were able to get the union leaders arrested. The growers also shut down the union meeting places in certain parts of California. Over time, the IWW began to splinter into regional groups, which went their own ways. Eventually the lack of an overall leadership resulted in the IWW's loss of much of its influence. The union still exists today, but its membership is much smaller than it was during the IWW's heyday in the early 20th century.

Sometimes, the resistance to unions came from other migrants. White migrant workers often carried their own prejudices and hatred with them when they moved from Texas, Oklahoma, and Arkansas. Even during the Great Depression, some white laborers refused to work with the nonwhite migrants—even though all the migrants were equally poor and desperate.

During part of the Great Depression, Jessie de la Cruz was a 13-year-old Mexican migrant worker. Her days were spent bent over a large cloth bag as she cleaned cotton. For this work, she earned 10 cents an hour. She recalled later how some of the white workers treated her and other Mexican workers:

> *They wouldn't even talk to us. We were ... living under the same conditions, but they thought they were better than we were.*

There was conflict among the different ethnic groups of nonwhite farmworkers as well. Whatever its source, the growers saw this conflict and used it for their own benefit. For example, if a Filipino workers' organization tried to negotiate for better wages, the growers would simply fire the Filipino workers and hire white or Mexican migrants to take their places. Throughout much of the early 1900s, the various ethnic groups did not work together toward their common goals.

Even though they continually met opposition from the growers, farmworkers still tried to use the power of the unions to fight for their basic rights as workers. One of the most common union-organized bargaining tools was the strike. The farmworkers would refuse to do any work until the growers met their demands.

Fruits and vegetables must be harvested within a certain period of time or the crop will be ruined. If the crop is ruined, the grower loses all the potential profit from that crop. Striking farmworkers hoped that the threat of losing the crop would force the growers to agree to the farmworkers' demands. Of course, while the farmworkers were striking they

In the 1930s, groups of Mexican workers started holding strikes as a way of fighting for better working conditions.

35

earned no money, which increased their hardship. The workers were committed to improving their lives, though, so they would use the strike in the hopes that the growers would pay attention to the farmworkers' demands.

The growers' response to strikers was to bring in other migrant workers, known as strikebreakers,

Growers brought in busloads of strikebreakers, or scabs, to replace workers who were on strike.

or scabs. Many people were desperate to work, and for each farmworker who walked off the job, there were several ready to take his or her place. The growers would simply replace any of the striking migrant workers with scabs.

In their hearts, many strikebreakers supported the idea of a farmworkers' union, but they felt they had to work in order to survive. In addition, most workers did not believe that a union of nonwhite workers would ever be able to win against the powerful and wealthy growers.

As the Great Depression tightened its grip on the United States in the mid-1930s, the growers cut wages even more. In 1933, a worker earned 40 cents for every 100 pounds (45 kg) of cotton he or she picked. Just a few years earlier, the rate paid was $1 for the same amount of cotton.

The cut in wages led the Cannery and Agricultural Workers Industrial Union to call a strike against the cotton growers in the San Joaquin Valley in central California. Both white and nonwhite workers walked off the fields. They formed picket lines to try to prevent strikebreakers from entering the fields. The farmworkers requested higher wages and asked that the growers recognize the union as the rightful representative of the farmworkers.

The growers responded to the strike with

In 1933, striking farmworkers encouraged other laborers in the fields to support a cotton pickers' strike that included 12,000 workers.

violence. They called on the police, who threw striking farmworkers out of the shacks in which they were living. The shacks, said the growers, were on their land. Entire families were evicted, with nowhere to go for shelter.

Some of the growers formed armed vigilante

groups, such as the Associated Farmers. The vigilantes took it upon themselves to punish those they saw as lawbreakers. One of these vigilante groups attacked some strikers gathered outside a union meeting hall. When the vigilantes finished shooting, strikers Delores Hernandez and Delfino Davila were dead, and several others were wounded. Even though 11 growers were arrested, none were convicted.

ASSOCIATED FARMERS

The Associated Farmers was an organized group of growers in the Imperial Valley of California. They joined together to fight the newly forming unions in any way they could. Often resorting to violence, they controlled vigilante groups that used guns, tear gas, and beatings to crush any strike called by a union.

Violence exploded throughout the 1930s and 1940s as farmworkers tried—again and again—to organize into unions. Strikers were often beaten. The growers tried to drive a wedge between the small unions by encouraging them to compete against one another for jobs.

The growers had local government officials on their side. In Kern County, north of Los Angeles, one sheriff said:

> *We protect our farmers here in Kern County. They are our best people. They are always with us. They keep the county going. They put us here and they can put us out again, so we serve them.* ◣

A Leader From the Fields

Chapter 4

While farmworkers struggled to organize into a union during the Great Depression, a young migrant boy named Cesar Chavez was growing up working in the fields. He was a Mexican-American who had been born on his family's farm near Yuma, Arizona. Like many other families, though, the Chavez family lost their farm during the Depression. Soon after they lost their land, the family joined more than 300,000 other people in following the harvests in California.

Cesar was 11 years old when he became a migrant worker. Losing the family farm had been hard on him and his elder sister, Rita. Cesar knew it must have been even harder on his parents. Members of the Chavez family had never worked for another person. They had owned a home and farm animals. The Chavez children had played on open land as far as the eye could see. In 1933, however, their world had suddenly changed. Cesar later remembered, "We left everything behind. Left chickens and cows and horses and all the implements ... everything."

When they became migrant workers, the Chavez family met with the same abuses that previous migrants had experienced. They were, for example, cheated out of wages after working long hours in

Cesar Chavez grew up during the Great Depression.

the sun. Even though Cesar and his siblings were children, they did a full day's work if jobs could be found. Times were so hard that everyone's work was needed to help put food on the family's table. When they worked in the lettuce fields, they spent hours twisting their bodies this way and that in order to use a special, short-handled hoe. Then, at the end of each tiring day, they were reminded that they no longer had a real home. "We were lucky we got a tent. Most of the time we were living under a tree, with just a canvas on top of us," Cesar's sister Rita said.

Cabbage pickers, like many other farmworkers in the 1930s, used tools that required the workers to spend most of the day bent over.

El Cortito

Migrant workers who toiled in the sugar beet and lettuce fields were forced to use a special tool. It was a short-handled hoe that they called *El Cortito*, "the short one." This special hoe had a handle that was only 12 or 18 inches (30.5 or 45.7 centimeters) long. A regular hoe has a long handle that allows a person to stand up while using it. El Cortito, however, forced workers to stay in a bent-over position, twisting their bodies to crawl along rows of lettuce or beets. After 10 or 12 hours of holding this position, many people were unable to stand straight. Because the children's bones were still forming, using El Cortito was especially harmful for them. It often resulted in horribly painful backaches for the rest of their lives. Even though the long-handled hoe could be used, the growers insisted that workers use El Cortito. The growers believed that the short-handled tool caused less damage to the growing vegetables.

Each day that he worked, Cesar learned more and more. He noticed everything around him, especially the poor treatment of migrant workers. He saw that the growers had power and that the migrant workers had none. They were almost like slaves. Cesar believed that because his family had once owned land, they were more willing to stand up to the injustices they saw. He said:

> *Some [farmworkers] had been born into the migrant stream. But we had been on the land, and I knew a different way of life. We were poor, but we had liberty. The migrant is poor, but he has no freedom.*

Like Cesar and his siblings, Mexican-American migrant children often faced hurtful racism while working in the fields.

The Chavez family had not been migrant workers all their lives. They knew that there was another way to live. This gave Cesar and his family the courage they needed to survive. Cesar believed that all migrant workers deserved to know a better life. He promised himself that someday they would.

Cesar watched how his father, Librado, responded to unfairness or mistreatment while working in the fields. Librado was a quiet man, but he would not allow anyone to treat him, or a member of his family, like a slave. In the field, when supervisors tried to cheat them, Librado would gather his family and walk off the job. He would do this even if it was the most important time to be picking cotton or vegetables.

The Chavez family would then look elsewhere for work. Cesar's father joined different unions as they came along. Librado always supported the union-led strikes for better wages and working conditions. Cesar remembered that his family was the first to walk off a field if someone called a strike. He later explained:

> It [the inclination to support the strike] didn't come to us because we knew anything about labor. It came to us because it was the right thing to do.

Because they were migrant workers, Cesar and his brothers and sisters went to many different schools. Cesar attended 36 different schools while his family worked as migrant laborers. Like other nonwhite migrant children, Cesar faced humiliation and the hurtful words of the other students. He was called a "dirty Mexican" on more than one occasion. Even though those experiences were painful, Cesar learned that education for migrant children was an important right—a right they did not yet have.

45

The abuses migrant workers such as the Chavez family faced were not just limited to the fields. Cesar and his family saw many signs outside restaurants and stores that said White Trade Only. Cesar's father was thrown out of a café simply for ordering a cup of coffee. Mexicans were not allowed to eat or drink in that café. Cesar never forgot the look on his father's face. It strengthened Cesar's will to bring about social change in the United States.

When Cesar was in the eighth grade, Librado was in a serious car accident and for a long time was unable to work. Cesar decided that he would quit school and take his father's place as the main worker in the family. Although his parents were against the idea, Cesar insisted. Soon Cesar began reading everything about unions he could get his hands on. He believed that unions could do much to help migrant workers.

By 1952, Cesar Chavez was a married man and a father. After serving his country in World War II, he had returned to California and was working in a lumberyard in San Jose. His goals now included fighting for the rights of the Mexican-American people, no matter where they worked.

Chavez learned about an organization called the Community Service Organization (CSO). Fred Ross, a man who would become his teacher and lifelong friend, met with Chavez to tell him about the CSO and its mission. Ross called himself an organizer. He worked with the CSO in Los Angeles,

CESAR'S HEROES

Cesar Chavez was influenced by books he read about people who had helped change the societies of their times. These people included St. Francis of Assisi and labor leader Eugene Debs. Francis of Assisi was a wealthy man who became a priest and dedicated his life to helping the poor. Eugene Debs organized the American Railway Union, one of the first industrial unions in the United States. He was later one of the founders of the Industrial Workers of the World union. Chavez also read the works of the person who would most influence his later work as a union leader—Mohandas Gandhi. He was a leader in India's fight for independence from Great Britain. Most important, Gandhi firmly believed in nonviolence as an effective way to change society. A commitment to nonviolence would become one of Chavez's strongest tools in his fight for the rights of migrant workers.

where he had helped residents fight for their rights as citizens. The CSO helped people get the city to clean up the polluted canal in which children played. The group had also helped change the laws keeping white and nonwhite people separated in stores and public places. Ross was looking for someone within the Mexican-American community in San Jose who would act as a leader in getting Mexican-Americans registered to vote. He was sure Chavez was that man.

Chavez started working with the CSO. He went door-to-door in his neighborhood getting the residents involved in voting registration and community projects. He met other people as committed to the civil rights of those in the community as he was himself. Dolores Huerta was a teacher and a mother. She had grown up

47

Cesar Chavez worked with the Community Service Organization to help register Mexican-Americans to vote.

48

in Stockton, California, where her mother ran a boardinghouse. Like Chavez, she was particularly interested in helping farmworkers. Huerta became a close associate and was one of Chavez's most trusted friends.

Chavez worked with the CSO for 10 years. During that time, his mind often returned to the suffering of the migrant farmworkers. He wanted to extend to them the help that an organization like the CSO could provide. Chavez knew firsthand exactly what migrant farmworkers faced. He knew the obstacles, but he believed they could be overcome. Doing so would take persistence and hard work.

In his mind, Chavez imagined a union that involved all the workers in making decisions. He dreamed of migrant workers from all cultures and areas of the country finally being treated with fairness and respect. Chavez believed this could happen. With the right people working together, life for migrant workers could change. ◣

La Causa

In 1962, Cesar Chavez made a decision that forever changed his life and the lives of many other people. He left the Community Service Organization to begin organizing the National Farm Workers Association. The goal of improving the lives of all farmworkers became known as *La Causa*, meaning "The Cause."

The years Chavez had spent in the CSO had taught him different ways to persuade those in authority to listen to what he had to say. He had studied the methods of other civil rights leaders, such as Mohandas Gandhi and Martin Luther King Jr. Chavez had watched how King had acted in trying to achieve civil rights for African-Americans. King had shown that nonviolence could be a powerful way of achieving a goal. Chavez saw that quiet but determined protest could be effective.

Dolores Huerta, Cesar Chavez, and other leaders in the Mexican-American community announced the organization of the new National Farm Workers Association.

The NFWA would fight for the farmworkers' right to a fair wage. It would fight for their right to safe working conditions. The new union would fight for all the things farmworkers needed.

There were already some organizations and unions fighting for the rights of farmworkers, such as the Agricultural Workers Organizing Committee (AWOC). These groups tried, but they were not successful in winning a permanent solution to the farmworkers' problems. For example, the unions might win an increase in wages for a short time, but the increase did not last. There was still no insurance for farmworkers injured on the job—a benefit that workers in most other industries had had for many years. Large national unions such as the American Federation of Labor and the Congress of Industrial Organizations, known together as the AFL-CIO, had largely ignored the farmworkers.

Chavez hoped the NFWA would force the growers to meet with the farmworkers face-to-face. Then he wanted the growers to come to an agreement on the farmworkers' demands. Chavez knew that forming this union successfully would take years of hard work and patience. He later said, "What I didn't know was that we would go through hell because it was all but an impossible task."

Chavez believed that the NFWA would have the best chance of success in Delano in California's San Joaquin Valley. In that community were migrant workers from various ethnic groups—Mexicans, Filipinos, African-Americans, and Caucasians. Chavez knew that the different groups often ended up competing with one another for work or housing. The growers used the farmworkers' disunity to keep the groups at odds with one another. Chavez recognized that as long as each group pursued only its own limited goals, the farmworkers as a whole would never win against the growers. The farmworkers had to work together to pursue one goal—a union that represented all of them.

In the early 1960s, most migrant farmworkers following crops in the United States were Mexicans or Chicanos (people of Mexican heritage who are born and grow up in the United States). Chavez and

Chavez held meetings to discuss the best ways to involve Mexican and Chicano workers in the NFWA.

53

Dolores Huerta first took the NFWA's message to the Spanish-speaking farmworkers. Gilberto Padilla and Julio Hernandez joined Chavez and Huerta in bringing the union's message to the farms.

Luis Valdez was another Chavez supporter in the early days of the farmworkers' union. He shared Chavez's passion for improving the lives of farmworkers. Valdez wrote skits that presented the issues the farmworkers faced. He said:

In 1962, at the National Farm Workers Association's first convention, Dolores Huerta signed up new members.

> *Here was Cesar, burning with patient fire, poor like us, dark like us, talking quietly, moving people to talk about their problems ... always suggesting—never more than that—solutions which seemed attainable. We didn't know it until we met him, but he was the leader we had been waiting for.*

For months, Chavez and the members of the NFWA traveled throughout the San Joaquin Valley. They spoke to the farmworkers in the fields and in their homes. They spoke to them anywhere they could. Some of the farmworkers were impressed by how hard the NFWA people worked to understand the farmworkers' opinions on important issues. No other union had done that before. Soon farmworkers were seeking out Chavez and asking for his help. Could Chavez help them with stolen wages? Could the NFWA help with the costs of burying a relative? In each case, Chavez and the NFWA did whatever they could. They wanted to prove to all the farmworkers that a union could work if everyone pulled together. Chavez had told his associates to "get information directly from the workers and find out how they feel on some of those questions that outsiders have been deciding for the workers for too ... long."

On September 30, 1962, about 200 farmworkers and their families gathered at an empty movie theater in Fresno, California. These farmworkers were the representatives of even more farmworkers. Chavez had an exciting proposal for them. If the farmworkers agreed, the NFWA would be their representative in trying to get the rights they deserved. The NFWA would start working with the government of California to persuade it to establish $1.50 as the lowest hourly wage a farmworker could earn. At the time, the hourly wage was often $1 or less. The NFWA would also present the idea that it had the right to negotiate with the growers on behalf of the farmworkers. Until then, the growers did not recognize any group as representing all the farmworkers. The farmworkers had never been asked to vote directly on the issues that would affect their lives. They voted in favor of the NFWA's ideas. Chavez was elected president of the association. Dolores Huerta, Gilberto Padilla, and Julio Hernandez were elected vice presidents.

During the next two years, NFWA membership slowly grew. In 1965, the organization had a chance to show the farmworkers what a united group could do. Padilla, as part of the NFWA, accused the state of California of making a profit from labor camps that were in terrible condition. Migrant workers had to live in these camps that were originally built in the 1930s for workers during the Great Depression. Many workers were forced to live in shacks that had no running water. They were so poorly built that they offered little protection from the weather. The current migrant workers paid rent to live in these shacks, and the state of California was planning on raising the rent.

The NFWA organized marches to protest this plan. They started a rent strike that lasted all summer. The workers refused to pay rent as long as the shacks remained in such terrible condition. Because the workers remained united during these actions, the government officials responsible for the camps were forced to respond. They made repairs and improved the housing in the camps. The NFWA had won its first battle for the farmworkers.

The NFWA was growing slowly, and it needed time to gain strength. But events pushed the union to take a bigger action than it had planned. In 1964, the large growers were sure that there would not be enough workers for the harvest. They pressured the U.S. government to allow them to use guest workers from Mexico.

The situation became worse for farmworkers farther north in the San Joaquin Valley. Growers in Coachella, California, offered only $1 an hour to the Filipino farmworkers. The leaders in AWOC knew that if the Filipino workers went on strike, the growers would simply replace Filipino workers with local Mexican and Chicano workers. The Filipino laborers needed the support of the NFWA if they were to succeed in their strike. Even though the NFWA was not as powerful as Chavez knew it would be someday, it joined with the Filipino workers in their strike. This was the first time that the Filipino, Mexican, and Chicano farmworkers joined in such a large

BRACEROS

Guest workers from Mexico were called *braceros*, which is Spanish for "arms." They had been an important part of the U.S. labor force during World War II. The agreement with the Mexican government was that the braceros would earn at least $1.40 per hour. The growers honored that agreement but then offered the workers who were already living and working in the fields only $1.25 per hour. Most of these workers were Filipino, and they belonged to the Agricultural Workers Organizing Committee (AWOC). They were experienced farmworkers and would not agree to work for 15 cents less an hour than the guest workers. The AWOC farmworkers went on strike.

effort. This strike was an important action, and everyone involved knew it. One of the older Mexican farmworkers was an immigrant. He said:

> *It is an honor to come here and we must not abuse it. We are all humans, and we have to aid our brothers the Filipinos in this just cause. Let's go out on strike!*

The strike came to be called the Great Delano Grape Strike. With the Mexican and Filipino farmworkers united, 48 farms would face the strike. About 2,000 workers walked out. This meant that about 450 square miles (1,170 square km) of vineyards would not be harvested if the growers declined to meet the demands of the strikers. The growers refused to give in. They brought in strikebreakers from other places to cross the union picket lines. The strikebreakers included children, who worked under the watchful eye of an armed sheriff's deputy.

Chavez knew that news of the farmworkers' struggle had to be told all across the nation. He believed that if people knew about the hardships the farmworkers faced, they would care. Chavez and the NFWA members invited newspaper and television reporters to document the strike.

The AFL-CIO publicly supported the NFWA strike. The AFL-CIO member unions represented almost all unionized workers in the United States. By supporting the NFWA strike, the AFL-CIO

was telling its membership that it believed the farmworkers deserved the rights for which they were fighting.

Little did anyone know that the strike would last many months. That meant months without money coming in for the farmworkers' families. It meant months of resisting the growers, the strikebreakers, and even some of the local police. The challenge of keeping the farmworkers' spirits up and committed to the strike fell to the NFWA leadership. Whatever it took, they could not let the farmworkers lose heart. ◣

59

The Grape Boycott Begins

In December 1965, the NFWA took yet another step. It called for a boycott on a particular company—Schenley Industries. This corporation controlled miles of vineyards. Its products included many different brands of liquor. The NFWA asked the American public to stop buying anything produced by Schenley Industries until the company agreed to the union's demands.

The strike grew. It spread to include volunteers picketing the warehouses where the grapes were stored. They also picketed at the docks from which the grapes would be shipped. Members of other unions sometimes honored the strike by refusing to load the grapes onto the ships. Volunteers traveled to more than 100 cities in the United States to spread the word about the grape boycott. They made sure that the public

Supporters of the grape boycott took the message to grocery stores in cities across the United States.

BOYCOTT GRAPES
BOYCOTT GRAPES
UNFAIR
to organized Labor
UFWOC AFL-CIO
Do Not Patroniz
This Store Sells
Grapes
UFWOC
THIS STORE
UNFAIR
TO ORGANIZED
LABOR
AFL-CIO

HELP FROM THE COMMUNITY

Churches and social groups stepped up to help the striking workers. They collected food and clothing and gave them to the farmworkers. The United Auto Workers union voted to donate $5,000 each month to help the NFWA and AWOC strikers for the duration of the strike.

knew that Schenley Industries had union contracts for its truck drivers and some warehouse workers. There was no union contract for the farmworkers, though, and the NFWA was determined to change this fact.

As the months passed, the pressure on the farmworkers and on the NFWA leaders to give in to the growers was strong. The strikers ran out of money to buy food. It was hard to stay committed to a strike when your family was going hungry. The strikers worried that they would be unable to pay rent and medical bills. However, the determined members of the NFWA had earned the group some friends in the area.

The strikers also had supporters in the media and in politics. In March 1966, a U.S. Senate subcommittee on migratory labor held hearings in Delano. Senator Robert Kennedy of New York was one of the panel members to hear Chavez and representatives of the California farming businesses. They presented their views of the conditions in which migrant workers lived. Chavez spoke for the farmworkers. He said:

Ranchers in Delano say that the farmworkers are happy living the way they are—just like the Southern plantation owner used to say about the Negroes.

The farm business owners expected Senator Kennedy and the others on the panel to support the growers. Instead, Kennedy came out in support of the farmworkers. He even joined Chavez and other workers on a picket line. The newspaper and television reporters made sure that Americans across the nation saw Kennedy's show of support for the farmworkers.

Even though the farmworkers were seeing growing support for their cause, it was easy to become discouraged. The day-to-day struggle of trying to make ends meet was hard to bear. As time went on, some of the farmworkers simply gave up and left the area. Chavez and the NFWA knew that they needed to take some type of special action that would help keep the farmworkers united. The action would also serve to keep the focus of the American people on the farmworkers' struggle.

One of the union members suggested holding a protest march. This wouldn't be like any other protest march, though. The marchers would walk more miles than any other marchers in the United States had ever walked. A protest march like this would surely make the American people aware of the farmworkers' cause. The union chose March 17 as the day the march would begin.

63

With flags and banners raised high, the marchers began the long trip from Delano to Sacramento.

Volunteers would walk almost 300 miles (480 km) from Delano to the Capitol in Sacramento. They would walk every step, in all types of weather, and they would do it in time to arrive in Sacramento on Easter Sunday, April 10, 1966.

The march would be a pilgrimage, like those of religious pilgrims of centuries past. The marchers would make stops at small farm towns along the way. They would pray and lift the spirits of the striking farmworkers. This would also lift the spirits of the farmworkers who watched the marchers as they made their way to Sacramento.

The march would take place at the end of Lent, which precedes the Christian holiday of Easter. For many Christians, Lent is a time of sacrifice and penance. It is a time of making amends and receiving forgiveness. Chavez was a religious man, and the idea of completing the march on Easter Sunday—the day commemorating Christ's Resurrection—was deeply symbolic. Resurrection was a symbol of change. The theme of the march became Pilgrimage, Penance, and Revolution.

Chavez led the march as it left Delano. Angie Hernandez Herrera walked close to Chavez. There were about 100 people at the beginning of the march. Several marchers carried the NFWA banner, with its black eagle on a red background. The symbol would inspire the marchers during the weeks to come.

The people in the march knew they were making history. They felt united and powerful in the belief that their actions would lead to positive change. As Chavez had told them, "There is no power in the world like the power of free men working together in a just cause."

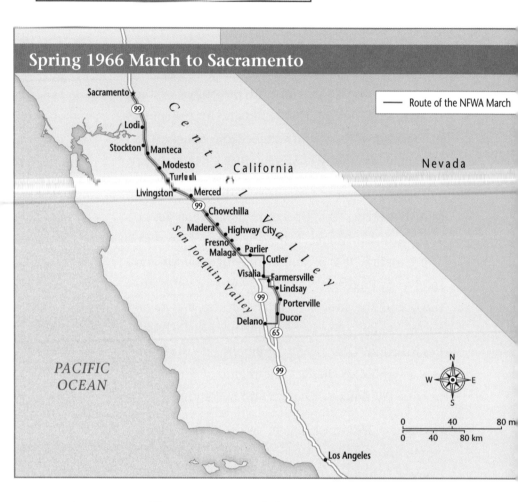

Spring 1966 March to Sacramento

Route of the NFWA March

Sacramento
99
Lodi
Stockton | Manteca
Modesto
Turlock
Livingston
Merced
99
Chowchilla
Madera
Highway City
Fresno
Malaga
Parlier
Cutler
Visalia
Farmersville
Lindsay
99
Porterville
Delano
Ducor
65
99

California

Nevada

Central Valley

San Joaquin Valley

PACIFIC OCEAN

N
W E
S

0   40   80 m
0   40   80 km

Los Angeles

The route the marchers took from Delano to Sacramento was just under 300 miles (480 kilometers).

The excitement of the marchers extended into the towns and cities they passed through. Often local farmworkers and community members would provide enough food and drink for all the marchers. At night, the marchers stayed with local families who had opened their homes. The marchers were weary after walking as far as 15 miles (24 km) a day. Still, the support of the people they met gave them the courage and strength to continue the march the next day.

WE'RE WATCHING YOU

Newspapers, television, and radio are powerful communication tools. Cesar Chavez relied on the media to communicate his nonviolent efforts to win basic rights for farmworkers. Television and newspaper reporters documented almost every step of the march to Sacramento. Media coverage greatly influenced how the farmworkers themselves acted and, often, how others acted toward them. During the civil rights movement, images of violence were shown throughout the country. Americans saw that law enforcement officers and others often treated peaceful marchers cruelly. Viewers also witnessed the actions of supporters who tried to help the civil rights workers.

Television and newspaper reporters followed Chavez and the marchers to document the event. Media coverage inspired Americans around the nation to act. On April 4, about 250 Chicago residents marched peacefully through some of the local Mexican and Puerto Rican neighborhoods in support of the migrant farmworkers. The march also inspired people nationwide to write to their newspapers expressing their opinions on the efforts of a group of people thousands of miles away.

As Chavez and the NFWA leaders had hoped, the march was getting the American public interested in the farmworkers' struggle. A few days before Easter, Chavez learned just how well the boycott and strike were working. Schenley Industries was ready to talk with the NFWA. After a few days of discussion, Schenley signed an agreement that met some of the farmworkers' demands. More

67

Carrying flags and banners, the marchers arrived in Sacramento. important, Schenley formally accepted the NFWA as the official representative of the farmworkers who labored in the Schenley fields.

The Schenley victory was a major success for Cesar Chavez and the NFWA. Here was something that for so long they had only dreamed about. The marchers' efforts had paid off, and they arrived in Sacramento to cheers and celebrations.

When Chavez spoke to the crowd in Sacramento, he thanked the other unions, the community groups, and the volunteers who had helped the farmworkers win the victory against Schenley. He was proud of everyone's efforts. However, he also had another message: "It is well to remember that there must be courage, but also that in victory there must be humility."

He reminded the marchers that they had achieved just one victory. There were many growers like Schenley that would have to be dealt with one at a time. The farmworkers would have to win each victory. There was a great deal of work ahead for all of them. ◣

National Action

The DiGiorgio Corporation was one of the largest farming businesses in California. It also controlled the well-known Tree Sweet brand of fruit juices and the S&W brand of canned foods. DiGiorgio was a powerful company that had a lot of influence within the California government. Because it was so large, it employed hundreds of farmworkers.

Chavez knew it was important to get the union into DiGiorgio. This would be difficult, though, because DiGiorgio was known as a company that had fought hard against unions in the past. Chavez later recalled, "We were facing a giant whose policy was to break legitimate unions."

Under the watchful eyes of the police, strikers called on field workers to support a walkout.

Even so, the small NFWA pitted itself against the giant called DiGiorgio. Chavez knew that the NFWA would need to rely on a strategy that DiGiorgio would not expect.

The NFWA had found success with nonviolent boycotts and strikes. The union decided to continue using those tools but with a difference: It would call boycotts and strikes throughout all of DiGiorgio's many locations. In this way, the company would feel the effect of the boycotts and strikes more quickly.

In San Francisco, NFWA supporters picketed stores carrying DiGiorgio brand foods. They also picketed the warehouses where the food was stored. And they picketed the DiGiorgio Corporation's headquarters. In Chicago, NFWA supporters blocked an S&W Foods distribution center. This location delivered S&W canned products throughout the Midwest. Many truck drivers from the Teamsters union sided with the NFWA. The drivers would not cross the picket line. The result was that none of the products could be delivered to stores. If the products weren't on the store's shelves, they couldn't be sold.

The DiGiorgio Corporation did not expect such widespread activity in support of the farmworkers. During the previous months, DiGiorgio had used its own influence to get court orders that limited the number of picketers who could demonstrate at any company-owned location. The company brought in strikebreakers from Texas and Mexico

to the DiGiorgio fields in California. While the DiGiorgio representatives were discussing changes with the NFWA, they were continuing to try to block the union's efforts.

DiGiorgio bused in strikebreakers to work in its fields when unions went on strike.

DiGiorgio even tried to pit different unions against one another. The corporation's leaders believed that if the unions fought one another, DiGiorgio could continue to do business as it always had.

In response to DiGiorgio's efforts to pit the unions against one another, the groups combined forces. As a result, the NFWA joined with the AWOC to become a new, bigger, and stronger organization—the United Farm Workers Organizing Committee (UFWOC). This group eventually became the United Farm Workers (UFW).

The boycott and strikes quickly caused the DiGiorgio Corporation to lose money. In November 1966, DiGiorgio allowed its farmworkers to vote for a union to represent them. The workers chose the UFWOC. The contract that the union worked out with DiGiorgio was the first to provide a health and welfare fund that was paid for by the company instead of the farmworkers. And, for the first time, farmworkers had paid vacations and holidays.

Chavez (seated center) exchanges pens with John Giumarra Sr., who represented 26 of California's grape growers, as they agree to a union contract.

These were miraculous gains for workers who before the strikes had not been allowed to even take a break during the workday to get a drink of water. Equally important, workers could not lose their

jobs simply because they supported a union.

However, other growers soon stepped into the fight against a farmworkers' union. The Giumarra Vineyards was one of the largest grape-growing businesses in California. Like DiGiorgio, Giumarra fought hard to keep the farmworkers from organizing a union. In August 1967, the Giumarra workers voted to strike. The grower had about 5,000 employees. Of these, more than 3,000 walked away from the fields in the middle of the harvest. Giumarra responded by bringing in strikebreakers. The UFWOC called for a national boycott of Giumarra grapes.

Giumarra tried to get around the boycott. It worked with other growers to ship its grapes under different labels. Giumarra hoped this practice would fool the union and the shoppers who supported the union. Shoppers on the other side of the country had no way of knowing whether they were buying Giumarra grapes, because the fruit might not carry the Giumarra label. The UFWOC would need to take yet another step in its ever-changing strategy.

In January 1968, Chavez and the UFWOC leaders decided to take an action that had never been taken before. Instead of boycotting just Giumarra grapes, the union called for a national boycott of all California table grapes. It wouldn't matter which farm they came from. There would be no confusion about whether the grapes in a store were from a boycotted farm. The grapes themselves would become a symbol of the farmworkers' struggle to improve their lives. The farmworkers asked everyone in the United States and Canada to stop eating grapes grown in California.

The boycott put the UFWOC up against the combined power of all the grape growers in California. The grape growers knew that a successful boycott would seriously hurt their businesses and, therefore, their profits. They were sure, however, that they would be able to beat the boycott because they had powerful allies in the government.

The growers most surely had powerful friends, and they had wealth. What they didn't have, however, were the hearts of people from all walks of life. The UFWOC decided that capturing the support of the American public would give it the power to overcome the growers.

PRESIDENTIAL DISAPPROVAL

In 1968, California Governor Ronald Reagan demonstrated his dislike of and lack of respect for the union by eating grapes in public. Even President Richard Nixon had said that he was against the grape boycott. To Cesar Chavez, those actions didn't matter. He said, "To us, the boycott of grapes was the most near-perfect of nonviolent struggles, because ... the whole essence of nonviolent action is getting a lot of people involved ... doing little things. ... A person can be persuaded not to eat a grape."

By July 1968, the UFWOC had identified 40 major cities in the United States and Canada that would serve as the focus areas for the union's efforts. Volunteers went to these cities to organize picket lines and communicate in a nonviolent way with anyone who would listen.

During 1969, volunteers distributed printed information that described the farmworkers' struggles. They set up picket lines at grocery stores and made signs to be carried during public marches. Men and women who had worked in the fields all their lives found themselves talking in crowded meeting halls filled with reporters and city leaders. Working on the picket lines, they found themselves

Chavez, carrying a sign calling for a boycott of California table grapes, leads about 400 people picketing a Safeway supermarket in Seattle, Washington, December 19, 1969.

asking perfect strangers to support their cause. One of these workers was Jesse Govea. She later recalled:

> *I saw these two young white men walking toward me. ... I made myself strong and went up to them and said, "Excuse me, could I ask you to help farmworkers by not buying grapes?" They both turned around and showed me their jackets, which had giant United Auto Workers emblems on them. And they turned around and said, "We're all for you. We're all for you."*

The growers recognized that they were witnessing a social movement unlike anything they had ever seen. Lionel Steinberg, a California grower, recalled:

> *This social, political boycott effort ... closed Boston, New York, Philadelphia, Chicago, Detroit, Montreal, Toronto completely from handling table grapes.*

In the summer of 1969, the growers went to court to sue the union. They claimed they had suffered $25 million in losses because of the grape boycott. By April 1970, the biggest grape grower in the Coachella Valley had signed a contract with the UFWOC. Within a few months, two more growers had signed contracts. On July 29, 1970, the UFWOC signed contracts with 29 grape growers.

Chavez and the farmworkers felt this was the beginning of a real change that would continue into the future. Chavez again spoke about his faith

At the end of the National Grape Boycott, farmworkers went back to work in the fields.

in nonviolent struggle to achieve a goal. He also spoke about how the farmworkers themselves had improved as people:

> *The strikers and the people involved in this struggle sacrificed a lot, sacrificed all of their worldly possessions. Ninety-five percent of the strikers lost their homes and their cars. But I think in losing those worldly possessions they found themselves.*

Chavez called an end to the National Grape Boycott in 1973. He had used the years between 1970 and 1973 to sign contracts with growers throughout California and Texas. During the years of the boycott, 17 million Americans were persuaded to stop buying grapes. It was the most successful boycott the United States had ever seen. ◣

A Continuing
Struggle

The National Grape Boycott focused the country's attention on farmworkers and the challenges they faced. Even though the grape boycott was successful, it was only the beginning of the farmworkers' fight to win workers' rights on all types of farms. One of the most important rights for them was to choose a union to represent them. Most farmworkers saw a union as the best way to win improvements in wages and benefits such as medical insurance.

The growers recognized this and continued to try to pit one union against another. They would pressure workers to join the union that the growers favored. Sometimes the growers simply would not sign a contract with the union the farmworkers wanted. Instead, they would sign a contract with another union that the growers chose. The relationship between the farmworkers, the unions, and the growers continued to be one of mistrust. Eventually, that mistrust exploded into violence.

In 1973, striking farmworkers in California's San Joaquin Valley faced violence from rival unions and the police. Two strikers died. Many more were severely beaten. It became obvious to the farmworkers that they needed more protection than just a contract with a grower.

As a result of the grape boycott, laws were passed in some states to protect the farmworkers' right to a union. In California, such a law was passed in 1975. It is called the Agricultural Labor Relations Act.

Local police handcuffed farmworkers and forced them off picket lines.

The enactment of this law was a great victory for the farmworkers.

Once again farmworkers hoped that they would be able to form a union without bloodshed. They soon learned, though, that the law would be difficult to enforce. The growers had many supporters within government. This meant the growers also had support among law enforcement officers. When conflicts took place, judges often tried to interpret the law to favor the growers.

Even though the battle was long, the farmworkers had achieved a great deal by the 1980s. Drinking water was available in the fields, and workers could stop to take a drink when they needed to. Their wages had improved enough so that some of them could afford to support their families. If a worker was hurt on the job, medical insurance would most likely help pay the bills.

Even so, in the 1980s, farmworkers still faced many challenges. One of the biggest challenges came in the form of new laborers coming in from Mexico. Most of these laborers were undocumented. The U.S. government did not know they were in the country, so they did not have a legal right to work in the United States. Even so, the extreme poverty in Mexico drove thousands of its residents to look for work in the United States.

Because these workers were in the United States illegally, they tried hard to avoid notice by law enforcement officials. The growers would hire immigrants to work in the fields for little pay. Wages were far lower than the rates documented workers received. The growers didn't have to worry about providing water or shelter, because they knew that the undocumented workers were too frightened to complain. If they did complain, they risked being sent back to Mexico.

CHILDREN IN THE FIELDS

Although laws were in place to prevent children from working, the ban was not enforced for Mexican immigrant children. Children 11 years old and younger spent their days crawling along the ground working in the fields. Since the farmworkers were in the country secretly, they would never complain. Many growers took advantage of the undocumented farmworkers' fears.

Laborers lived under trees or in caves they dug out of the soil. They were exposed to dangerous chemicals that were used to keep insects off of the fruit and vegetable plants. The spray made many farmworkers seriously ill.

In 1986, Congress passed the Immigration Reform and Control Act. For the first time, the hiring of undocumented immigrants for labor was illegal. The law also granted amnesty to hundreds of thousands of workers who were already living in the United States. All at once, illegal workers became legal workers. This law was a benefit to many of the farmworkers who worried about being sent back to the countries they had left. At the same time, the law was a threat to the farmworkers who were longtime residents of the United States and members of a union. The new arrivals became their

83

competition for jobs in the fields.

Today farmworkers face many of the same challenges they did during the last 40 years. The labor is hard and pays little. On average, a farmworker makes $6.82 per hour. This is less than what many employees at fast-food restaurants earn. More than half of all farmworker families live below the poverty level identified by the U.S. government. The hard work also means that most farmworkers have shorter lives and are more likely than many other types of workers to become ill. The majority of farmworkers have less education than other American workers. Often their formal education stopped at the sixth grade.

Approximately 83 percent of farmworkers who labor in American fields are of Hispanic descent. Some are U.S. citizens, but more than half of all farmworkers are undocumented. Like undocumented workers before them, they are not likely to complain if their working or living conditions are less than what they should be.

Children continue to work in the fields. The United Farm Workers union estimates that 800,000 children ages 17 and younger work in fruit and vegetable fields in the United States, picking the food that Americans eat. It is not unusual for children as young as 4 or 5 years old to work alongside their parents. Many children start full-time farm labor when they are 13 to 15 years old. These children join the migrant labor force for the summer months

before returning to school. Norma Flores recalled her childhood summers working along with the other members of her family: "Nothing can compare with being drenched in sweat and thirsty with an acre more of weeds to hoe in the middle of July."

Modern migrant farmworkers still work hard for low wages.

Documented farmworkers working in the fields today have more opportunities for government-sponsored education and health and medical benefits. For these farmworkers, life has improved a great deal from when Cesar Chavez began his work. For the undocumented farmworkers, however, time can stand still. Because they are afraid of being sent back to the countries they fled, they endure whatever they must in order to survive. As the United States tightens its policies on immigration, the undocumented farmworkers will be pressed even further. ◣

Timeline

1869

First transcontinental railroad is completed, making possible the shipment of California produce to markets throughout the United States.

1882

Congress passes the Chinese Exclusion Act, preventing further immigration from China.

1905

Industrial Workers of the World (IWW) forms, becoming one of the earliest labor unions.

1908

Japanese immigration to the United States is restricted, reducing the number of Japanese immigrants available to work as migrant farmworkers.

1917

Mexican immigrants begin legally arriving in the United States to work.

1923

Congress passes the Alien Land Law, making it illegal for immigrants who could not become citizens to own land.

March 31, 1927

Cesar Chavez is born in Arizona.

1932

Because of dust storms brought on by extended drought in the Midwestern states, thousands of American farmers lose their farms; many of these farmers head west to California to become migrant farmworkers.

1933

The Cannery and Agricultural Workers Industrial Union calls a strike against cotton growers in the San Joaquin Valley in California.

1939

Chavez, his parents, and his siblings arrive in California to become migrant farmworkers; John Steinbeck publishes *The Grapes of Wrath*, a novel that exposes the conditions in which migrant workers live.

1952

Chavez becomes a member of the Los Angeles Community Service Organization (CSO).

1959

The Agricultural Workers Organizing Committee (AWOC) is formed.

1962

Chavez forms the National Farm Workers Association (NFWA); its membership is made up largely of Mexican and Chicano farmworkers.

September 30, 1962

The NFWA is formally selected to represent the farmworkers in their negotiations with the California growers.

1964

The *bracero* program is reopened, bringing thousands of Mexican guest workers into the migrant stream.

September 1965

The NFWA and AWOC join to begin the largest farmworker strike in history, the Great Delano Grape Strike.

December 1965

The NFWA calls for a boycott on Schenley Industries, one of the largest California grape growers.

March 1966

Chavez attends a hearing on migratory labor held by a U.S. Senate subcommittee; Senator Robert F. Kennedy is a panel member.

March 17, 1966

Chavez leads a group of about 100 volunteers on a march from Delano, California, to the Capitol in Sacramento.

April 10, 1966

Chavez and the marchers arrive in Sacramento; Chavez announces that Schenley Vineyards has signed a contract recognizing the NFWA as the farmworkers' union.

August 3, 1966

AWOC and NFWA merge to become the United Farm Workers Organizing Committee (UFWOC).

April 1967

The UFWOC and DiGiorgio Fruit Corporation sign a contract giving the UFWOC the right to negotiate for its farmworker members.

August 1967

Approximately 3,000 employees of Giumarra Vineyards walk away from the fields in a strike; the UFWOC calls for a national boycott of Giumarra grapes.

Timeline

January 1968

The UFWOC calls for a national boycott of all California table grapes.

July 1968

Volunteers travel to major cities to spread the message of the grape boycott in locations ranging from neighborhood liquor stores to large grocery store chains.

July 29, 1970

A total of 29 growers negotiate contracts with the UFWOC. One of these growers is Giumarra Vineyards.

1972

UFWOC becomes the United Farm Workers (UFW).

1973

Chavez calls an end to the National Grape Boycott, the most successful boycott the United States had ever seen.

1975

California passes the Agricultural Labor Relations Act, which protects the farmworkers' right to form a union.

1986

Congress passes the Immigration Reform and Control Act; although it is now illegal to hire undocumented workers, the legislation grants legal or documented status to workers already in the United States.

On the Web

For more information on this topic, use FactHound.

1 Go to *www.facthound.com*

2 Type in this book ID: 0756524547

3 Click on the *Fetch It!* button. FactHound will find the best Web sites for you.

Historic Sites

California State Capitol Building
1400 10th St.
Sacramento, CA 95814
916/445-2841

Cesar Chavez and his supporters ended their 300-mile (480-km) march here in April 1966.

National Chavez Center at Nuestra Señora Reina de la Paz
29700 Woodford-Tehachapi Road
Keene, CA 93531
661/823-6134

This living memorial to Cesar Chavez includes exhibits that educate visitors abut his life, work, and values.

Look for More Books in this Series

The Berlin Wall:
Barrier to Freedom

The March on Washington:
Uniting Against Racism

Black Tuesday:
Prelude to the Great Depression

The Teapot Dome Scandal:
Corruption Rocks 1920s America

A Day Without Immigrants:
Rallying Behind America's Newcomers

Third Parties:
Influential Political Alternatives

Freedom Rides:
Campaign for Equality

A complete list of **Snapshots in History** titles is available on our Web site: *www.compasspointbooks.com*

Glossary

barrio
a Spanish-speaking community or neighborhood located within a U.S. city

boycott
to refuse to do business with someone as a form of protest

Caucasian
person who is of white European descent and not of Hispanic origin

embody
include

exclusion
stopping from entering

heyday
time of greatest success

industrialist
person who runs or owns a business related to the production of goods on a large scale

labor-intensive
requiring hard work

malnutrition
condition caused by an unhealthy diet

nonviolence
rejecting violence in favor of peaceful actions in achieving an objective

picket line
group of people gathered together in protest against a business

polluted
unfit or harmful to living things

prejudice
unfair treatment of a group of people who belong to a certain race or religion

racist
person who believes that one race is better than another

railroad baron
businessman who developed the railroads and as a result gained great wealth

restriction
limitation

resurrection
rising from the dead

Source Notes

Chapter 1
Page 10, line 19: Susan Ferriss and Ricardo Sandoval. *The Fight in the Fields: Cesar Chavez and the Farmworkers Movement.* New York: Harcourt Brace, 1997, p. 117.

Page 14, line 10: Ibid., p. 119.

Page 15, line 8: Ibid., p. 122.

Chapter 2
Page 24, line 21: Ibid., p. 26.

Chapter 3
Page 32, line 28: Ibid., p. 5.

Page 33, line 16: Ibid., p. 30.

Page 39, line 23: Ibid., p. 26.

Chapter 4
Page 41, line 4: Ibid., p. 17

Page 42, line 9: Ibid., p. 19.

Page 43, line 10: Ronald Taylor. *Chavez and the Farmworkers.* Boston: Beacon Press, 1975, p. 61.

Page 45, line 17: *The Fight in the Fields: Cesar Chavez and the Farmworkers Movement,* p. 30.

Chapter 5
Page 52, line 25: Jacques Levy. *Cesar Chavez: Autobiography of La Causa.* New York: W.W. Norton, 1975, p. 148.

Page 54, line 10: *The Fight in the Fields: Cesar Chavez and the Farmworkers Movement,* p. 113.

Page 55, line 16: Ibid., p. 71.

Page 58, line 4: Eugene Nelson. *Huelga: The First Hundred Days of the Great Delano Grape Strike.* Delano, Calif.: Farm Worker Press, 1966, p. 27.

SOURCE NOTES

Chapter 6
Page 63, line 1: *The Fight in the Fields: Cesar Chavez and the Farmworkers Movement*, p. 116.

Page 65, line 28: *Huelga: The First Hundred Days of the Great Delano Grape Strike*, p. 121.

Page 69, line 11: *The Fight in the Fields: Cesar Chavez and the Farmworkers Movement*, p. 123.

Chapter 7
Page 70, line 13: *Cesar Chavez: Autobiography of La Causa*, p. 222.

Page 76, sidebar: Ibid., p. 269.

Page 78, line 13: *The Fight in the Fields: Cesar Chavez and the Farmworkers Movement*, p. 149.

Page 78, line 15: *Cesar Chavez: Autobiography of La Causa*, p. 296.

Page 79, line 14: *The Fight in the Fields: Cesar Chavez and the Farmworkers Movement*, p. 157.

Chapter 8
Page 85, line 3: "*On the Border: Migrant Child Labor.*" PBS.org. 28 May 2004. Public Affairs Television. 13 December 2006. www.pbs.org/now/politics/FLORES.pdf

SELECT BIBLIOGRAPHY

Dunne, John Gregory. *Delano: The Story of the California Grape Strike.* New York: Farrar, Straus and Giroux, 1967.

Ferriss, Susan, and Ricardo Sandoval. *Fight in the Fields: Cesar Chavez and the Farmworkers Movement.* New York: Harcourt Brace, 1997.

Levy, Jacques. *Cesar Chavez: Autobiography of La Causa.* New York: W.W. Norton, 1975.

Nelson, Eugene. *Huelga: The First Hundred Days of the Great Delano Grape Strike.* Delano, Calif.: Farm Worker Press, 1966.

Ochoa, George. *Atlas of Hispanic-American History.* New York: Facts on File, 2001.

Taylor, Ronald. *Chavez and the Farmworkers.* Boston: Beacon Press, 1975.

FURTHER READING

Altman, Linda Jacobs. *Migrant Farm Workers: The Temporary People.* New York: Franklin Watts, 1994.

De Ruiz, Dana Catharine and Richard Larios. *La Causa: The Migrant Farmworker Story.* Austin, Texas: Raintree Steck-Vaughn, 1993.

Gonzales, Doreen. *Cesar Chavez: Leader for Migrant Farm Workers.* Springfield, N.J.: Enslow Publishers, 1996.

Haugen, Brenda. *Cesar Chavez: Crusader for Social Change.* Minneapolis: Compass Point Books, 2008.

Jiménez, Francisco. *The Circuit.* Abuquerque: University of New Mexico Press, 1997.

Index

About the Author

Barbara J. Davis has been writing children's nonfiction for more than 20 years. Her specialities are science, history, and nature topics. She lives in Hinckley, Minnesota. Her hobbies are reading, working with rescue dogs, and riding her horse, Wing.

Image Credits